# Red Pepper Black Pepper

Harmeet Kaur



Beco
Shake
.com

**First published in 2020 by**

**Becomeshakespeare.com**

One Point Six Technologies Pvt Ltd.
119-123, 1st Floor, Building J2, B - Wing,
WadalaTruck Terminal, Wadala East, Mumbai,
Maharashtra, India, 400022.
T: +91 8080226699



ISBN - 978-93-90463-21-3

**Dedicated to:**

my Dad S.Karamjeet Singh Bahri

# Acknowledgement

This collection of poetry is based more on my indefatigable experiences of life which I share with my husband Vikramjeet Singh Bhalla. My children Vishakha and Anmol have proved to be the true outcome of my work Red Pepper Black Pepper.

# Contents

## Section 1- Preaching



## Section 2 Nurturing

## Section 4 Appealing

# Preface

I feel "Poetry is an extravagant art of communication of thoughts which flow from the poets' mind like the tides of the ocean, forceful and tense and reach the readers' mind with a splash."

This collection of poetry is a compilation of my very true experiences of life. An infant is unknown and unaware of the world when it cradles in the mothers lap. The toddler nurtures, grows and breathes with its parents. The wavering period from becoming a teenager to an adult requires meticulously handling the grim situations. Every single day brings a new joy or sorrow. The youth of today should manage to swim across the overflowing river with zeal and confidence. They should be capable enough to face the challenges and have an optimistic approach to life.

As a parent give ample time and adoration to your child so that he walks alone with sincere thoughts on the road to success. The path may not be smooth, and it may have hurdles. You may rise and fall but stand again and rush towards your goal. The world is a magnificent place created by God and life is the most precious gift bestowed to mankind so value it. The three basic qualities struggle, sacrifice and sublimity if inculcated in mankind will help them to attain heights of success. Let us try to bring peace and prosperity in this world and make the world a better place to live in.

This book consists of four sections:

1. Preaching: Every religion has its sanctity and aura. The various religious leaders have tried to portray the authenticity of God's presence. They want human beings to develop humanitarian values and establish a true relationship with God. By reading the holy scriptures we grasp the essential elements and methods of culminating ourselves in this Universe. We are the children of God and our destiny is framed on the good and bad deeds done by us. Let us cherish each moment given by God and spread the message of generosity.

2. Nurturing: The red and black pepper theory is the simple way of inculcating values in kids. This gentle fear makes way for them in learning, speaking and becoming good. In the several stages which man comes across while residing in this world life never appears to be a bed of roses. The one who has a sincere upbringing will adjust in all circumstances. The fact lies in the way you accept the harsh realities of life. Learn to be a winner and climb every step with patience.

3. Enchanting: This section comprises of Haiku, a kind of poetry in which the message is conveyed in three lines. We should be grateful to God for giving us some of the most beautiful gifts of nature. The clouds, rain and the hues of the rainbow bring a magical influence on the people. The night sky seems to be like a balm and the seasons have their charm. We need to protect the birds and animals from getting extinct. Let mankind save the earth and the creatures.

4. Appealing: If we want to lead a dignified life, we have to value relationships. There are moments, human beings and breath-taking views which appeal to our heart and soul. Let these things make your life smooth and take you out from the depths of gloominess. Life will take an easy turn once you start living with these theorizations.

# *Section 1*
# PREACHING

# 1. Guru Nanak Devji

It happened some 550 years ago
It was the birth of a new religion
It was the birth of a Sikhism
In the year 1469, the village of Talwandi in Lahore
In the courtyard of Father Kaluchand and Mata Tripta
Was heard the squeal of Guru Nanak Devji
He possessed supernatural qualities since birth
People were surprised by seeing his mirth
The theory of Ek Om Kar was taught to mankind
He lifted the layman from the caste system
He preached the message of brotherhood
He wanted the rich to look towards the destitute
Leave your one slice of bread to fill their stomach
He said if Sikhs respected women
Their religion will be honoured by millions
He believed that if men did their business with honesty
They will gain more and more popularity
He pledged to save the air, water and earth

Today they all stand contaminated

Let us realize our Guru

Let us follow the path of our Guru

Let there be no gender differences

Let there be no caste dissimilarities

Dhan Guru Nanak, Dhan Guru Nanak, Dhan Guru Nanak.

# 2. Guru Gobind Singh Ji

The city of Patna became pious

In the year 1666 with the birth of Gobind Rai

Guru Teg Bahadur Ji and Mata Gujri Ji were blessed

At the age of nine, he attained Guruship

When his father was beheaded by the Mughals

A dashing warrior, poet and philosopher

A living God and a spiritual master

He had to save the nation from the downfall

To set standards for Sikhism he had a divine call

In 1699 he made the first Khalsa

After baptizing the first five he became the sixth Khalsa

A true Sikh will live with the five K's

Kachera, Kanga, Kara, Kirpan and Kesh

From Gobind Rai, he became Guru Gobind Singh Ji

'Kaur' is for females and 'Singh' for males

He fought several battles without fail

He didn't want to lose the country in the hands of the Mughals

His Zafarnama to Aurangzeb

Has set an example in the history of the Sikhs

The Holy Scriptures which he wrote

Takes us to a heavenly road

His ferocious four Singh's

Ajit Singh, Jujhar Singh, Zorawar Singh and Fateh Singh

Faced a tragic death in the hands of the Mughals

Guru Gobind Singh Ji was left with no successor

He breathed his last in Nanded in October 1708

He made the holy Guru Granth Sahib Ji the living Guru
his successor.

# 3. The Martyrdom

The history of the Sikhs holds an aura spectacular

We wholeheartedly pay homage to the four sons of Guru Gobind Singh Ji

The valiant, innocent and the ferocious four

Their martyrdom saved our country from the Mughals therefore

Baba Ajit Singh the unconquerable was born a Paonta Sahib

To Mata Sundariji when Guruji won the Battle of Bhangani

At Anandpur Sahib, he learnt history and philosophy

Baba Jiwan Singhji taught him swordsmanship and archery

In the second Battle of Chamkaur, he led his sallies

He was seventeen when he died in the hands of the enemies

Baba Jujhar Singh was born to Mata Jitoji at Anandpur Sahib

The dauntless and the generous was a true Khalsa

He got trained in the martial arts Gatka

In the second Battle of Chamkaur, he led the sally

He was fourteen when he died in the hands of the enemies

Baba Zorawar Singh was born to Mata Jitoji at Anandpur Sahib

The cold rivulet Sirsa separated him from his father

Gangu betrayed them and took them to the Mughals

Wazir Khan told the two to convert into Islam

He was bricked alive and beheaded

He was nine when he breathed his last

Baba Fateh Singh was born to Mata Jitoji at Anandpur Sahib

He was accompanied by his brother Zorawar Singh

Their grandmother Mata Gujri Ji dressed them up that morning

Her heart swelled with pride at their decision

They saved the country and shunned conversion to Islam

He was bricked alive and beheaded

He was seven when he breathed his last.

# 4. Lord Buddha

Amongst the gentle drizzle and blossoming flowers
In the garden of Lumbini in the bowers
The Prince was born with a strange destiny
All efforts were done to give him the luxury
He was moved by old age, death and misery
Siddhartha was married to Yashodhara
They had a son named Rahula
They shut him in the palace however
Still one night he moved out forever
He wanted to know the purpose of life
He practised meditation day and night
He moved towards spiritualism on seeing the plight
Lord Buddha the enlightened one gained insight
He was the founder of Buddhism
He preached the theory of non-violence
People can have control over their mind
If desires do not occupy or kill their time
He knows there is a cause for every suffering

Following non –attachment will bring an end to suffering
If we follow the teachings of Lord Buddha
The world will look like a splendid place forever.

# 5. Swami Vivekananda

The man with a mission
To enhance Hinduism
He gained spirituality
From Ramakrishna Paramhansa
He journeyed the world
To glorify his country
A place magnified
By Hindu mythology
The land was in chains
Under English, it remained
Freedom was the need
The people had to plead
He wanted to preach the world
With the Indian philosophies and Vedanta
A social reformer with a pure soul
Teachings he gave in plenty
He knew he would not live beyond forty.

# 6. Neem Karoli Baba

Together they pulled the chain

A man was thrown out of the train

Travelling without a ticket was not fair

He walked and vanished into the thin air

The train couldn't move for hours

All they required was a superpower

Passengers requested them to call the saint

The one thrown out was nowhere to be seen

The search for the holy man began soon

He lay beside the river in a swoon

He returned on one condition

At village Neem Karoli village they will build a railway station

The moment he stepped in the train

It started moving on the plain

"I do nothing, God does everything," said he

They all fell at his feet

He became Neem Karoli Baba from Maharajji

A worshipper of Lord Hanuman since birth
He knew why God had sent him on this earth
Seeing his devotion in plenty
His parents married him early
He left his house in search of God
He wanted to preach his message to all
"If you clean the mirror of your heart
You will see God"
People visited him from far and near
He blessed all and they became so dear
He searched for God from place to place
He got temples built at various places
"There is no religion, there is one God
and all religion leads to the same God" said he
He lived for years at Kainchi Dham
He breathed his last in Vrindavan.

# 7. Mother Teresa

A young girl from Skopje
On her visit to this country
Heard a celestial voice from the sky
To have a look at the diseased and needy
She made this foreign land her own
She decided never to return
Her heart did bleed for the poor
She made an open home for the destitute
She was a guardian to thousands of orphans
She hugged them tight and let them in
Her world was these children
She wiped them to look glistening
A commendable sacrifice of life
Mother Teresa left no stone unturned in her life.

# 8. Atheist or Theist

Unanswerable I stand at times with a strange question
When "Who is God?" is asked by the present generation
The explanation is unconventional
It has no beginning, end and middle
Our birth and death are still a mystery
It can be read in the books of mythology
There are various proofs to show
But the authentic ones are very low
His presence can only be felt
The greater will be the devotion
The more will be the realization
He is unseen and magnificent
The powerful and the omnipotent

Once you start practising meditation

Your mind becomes free from negative vibrations

You are surrounded by positivity

You manage serious things patiently

The choice is yours to become an atheist or theist

Do not follow the path of becoming an atheist

The plan of God is for the theist.

# 9. Tomorrow will always be a Surprise

In the coming seconds, minutes and hours
In the days, weeks and months
The future holds a surprise
Though we are never ready to compromise

I thought of going to the market
I couldn't go as I lost my jacket
I had decided to go to the temple
But I fell and broke my ankle

We build so many plans for future
But God's plan is always mature
We think about doing the best
He makes us calm and gives rest

No need to be in a hurry or panic
Maybe the path leads to something tragic
We wake up each morning with a bright sunrise
Tomorrow will always be a surprise.

# 10. Come to Me

O see with me believe in me
The world today tumbles
O taste with me enjoy with me
The delicacies present in nature
O hear with me give your ears
The sound of death and destruction
O touch with me press firmly thy hand
The poor and the destitute
O smell with me as it's hard to get the fragrance
Of the earth that lies like a wasteland
O come to me thy Lord
I stand diseased and paralyzed.

# 11. Keep Guiding Me All Day Long

I wake up each morning with flowers blooming
My mind elates on hearing the birds twittering
I am unknown and naïve on this earth to all
Keep guiding me all day long

The people surrounding me may be just or unjust
They may be falsifiers or trustworthy
It is complicated to judge them all along
Keep guiding me all day long

There may be innumerable who befool me
There may be few who take me off my track
There may be intruders who come along
Keep guiding me all day long

I may be sharing mistaken love with many

Faithful love may be far behind

Let only the dear ones come along

Keep guiding me all day long.

# 12. A Message from God

Last night I saw an uncanny dream

I saw myself crossing a crystal-clear stream

The water was somewhat frozen and ice-cold

I was empty-handed with nothing to hold

Beyond the stream there lay a passage

Two angels were standing as guards with a message

"A message From God" they said.

I stood aghast and stupefied by their beauty

"Your virtues and vice were counted"

"It is in heaven that you are wanted" said the angels

Their soft hands held mine

They took me inside in no time
"You're welcome to the passage to heaven," said they
The path looked so magnanimous
It seemed I was walking on cotton thus
The trees were loaded with flowers and fruits
The birds twittered on the treetops
So gentle and playful was the lamb
I ran to carry it in my arms
The feathered angels flew among the clouds
They waved at me and passed a smile
Will this be my new home now?
"Wake up child, why are you waving at me"
My mother woke me up with a smile
I rubbed my eyes and opened them wide
The Passage to heaven was nowhere in sight
But a message from God lay by my side

# 13. Exile

Lord Rama, Lakshmana and Devi Sita

Were on a journey to an unknown destination

They had been sent with hearts full of adoration

They were sent by mother Kaikiye on an exile of fourteen years

King Dashrath became helpless and perturbed

Bharat and Shatrughan wanted to accompany

Lord Rama refused them simply

They left their precious jewels and garbs

They went empty-handed without any words

The journey was tough and the path was rough

On the way, they crossed several rivers

They crossed and settled in various forests

The three faced many predicaments

Devi Sita got kidnapped by Ravana

She was saved by Hanuman

Lord Rama went on search of his life partner

Ravana and Lord Rama fought for several days

The fight ended with the death of Ravana
The Exile ended with a happy note
The people of Ayodhya rejoiced on their return
Flowers and lamps beautified the city
They celebrated the festival of Deepawali
The exile teaches us a lesson
That destiny of man is always hidden
Learn to be obedient and dignified
The Lord teaches us the way to gain magnificence.

▪

# 14. Gift of God

When I wake up with the sunrise every morning
I stand in front of the mirror smiling
I admire myself from head to toe
I exhibit myself to friends and foe
"Thank You, God" automatically comes out
I know there is nothing to feel proud
The body which we treasure is a blessing
Think of those who have something missing
The blind, deaf, dumb and lame
They too belong to the same clan
The plan of God is not the same in their life
They are devoid of the normal life
They too wanted to enjoy the ride
To have a future sumptuous with delight
We stand above all aloof and apart
So, let us cherish the gift of god.

# 15. Preaching

Praise the Lord from morning till night

Reach out to him in every aspect

Enthral the people with his name

Announce with joy and sing his name

Creator of heaven and earth

Heaven awaits the virtuous ones

Ignite the lamp in his glory

Names are several but God is one

God is the creator and the destroyer

# *Section 2*
# NURTURING

# 16. Red Pepper……Black Pepper

I always have two glistening bottles
In red and black on my table
All children are like beautiful flowers
We cannot shut them behind the bars

As coloured gems they are precious
Their upbringing is very tedious
Love your kids beyond limits
Never let them cross the limits

If they make petty mistakes
Black pepper should be on the plate
Either they have to eat themselves
Or promise to improve themselves

If they do serious mistakes
Red pepper should be on the plate
Either they will cry and plead
Or promise never to repeat

These small tricks make life so smooth
They imbibe good and decent values
Such children always outshine others
They always remember Red Pepper and Black Pepper.

# 17. First Mistake Last Mistake

To develop a stable and magnificent lifestyle
You need to set certain rules in your lifestyle
Upbringing is tough, at times we need to be rough
The sweetness and the charm are not always good

The young make hundreds of errors
There is always a certain kind of terror
The child is innocent like the lamb
You always have so many plans

The ladder to success is possible
At times you need to follow the impossible
Every single mistake is to be scrutinized
The life would otherwise be jeopardized

Whenever the first mistake is done
Try to be humble in return
Don't let your child be scared
Teach the difference between good and bad

Explain to him in several different ways
That the lord above watches your ways
The mistakes will later take you to hell
So, let the first mistake be the last mistake.

# 18. A New Beginning

You grow up as a normal kid
There may be times when you skid
Your upbringing was a challenge
Your parents spent sleepless nights
They never wanted you to go out of sight
You have always been a special child
Then why do you go wild
You decide to end your life
Without thinking of their strife
They live only for you
You live only for others

At times the gentle breeze did blow
Thunderstorms too were in the row
Don't live with a heart so tender
Be ready to face the blunder
Loosing is not an end
It is a new beginning
Live your life by being competent and bold
Life is given once so it is better to hold.

# 19. Untouchable

"Mother am I an untouchable," asked the child
The words pricked the heart of a mother
Born are all in the same row
Few still hold a degree low
Some crumbling customs still exist
They survive in dirt and filth
Back doors are open for them
The caste system is to be condemned
The garbage lying on the streets and in homes
Is picked by them which we have thrown
The job they do is to be praised
Their voices need to be raised
Let us change the present mindset
Let them possess the happiness that others get
Though they may have choices few
Don't make them feel blue.

# 20. Truth is Spoken Only Once

It is seen in all little girls and boys
They never pass their day without telling a lie
Every morning they get a lesson from their mother
Never to tell a lie another
In any subjects, if they have failed
They are afraid they will be scaled
Mothers should explain them gently
They should never hide even if they get a zero
By telling lies no one will become a hero
The journey of life is a long one
Times may come when you speak a lie to someone
The bitter truth will come out
No matter how many lies we shout
When we grow up to become a man or woman
Our faithfulness will make us a gentle person
Truth is spoken only once
For one lie you may speak a hundred
By telling lies let us not become corrupted.

# 21. Palaces and Huts

Lord never gives equality to humans
Each person is born with a different plan
Some are rich some poor
Some live-in palaces others in huts
There may be better chances of survival
If you become charitable
Your heart should melt on seeing the needy
Never ignore them as they are greedy
The world is full of feeble and diseased
They cry for help and they plead
Let us share little bread and butter
Let us teach each child to be better
These humanitarian values will flourish in them
It will make them superior and elegant
Let them get into caring and sharing
Open a new world for the destitute
Save them from becoming brute.

# 22. Women versus Women

The circumstances seem to be strange

When I see a woman deranged

All women are an enigma

All women have charisma

The seeds of enviousness are sown

It's hard to believe but it has grown

A woman abusing another woman

A woman mocking another woman

A woman thrashing another woman

A woman killing another woman

My heart aches on seeing this plan
I am bewildered on seeing this clan
In this world a Woman versus Woman
The men take advantage of this fact
They hardly follow this track
The women depict their narrowness
They should move towards the sacredness
Lend a helping hand to one another
Let none of the women suffer
Be humbler and more bent
Let all women have an idealistic temperament.

# 23. The Mask

Meeting a person for the first time
His impressions may be sublime
His gestures may be tolerant
As he is quite competent
One by one the layers peel off
Either he may rise or fall
Either he may moan or enthral
He is indeed wearing a thick mask
We should judge but never ask
It is better never to rely on a person soon
It takes ages to come out of the cocoon

Every bitterness will come out itself
May be there is goodness
Which he may present itself
He need not present his true self
Never in your life go on appearances
It will create only disturbances

# 24. Few Literates are Still Illiterates

It is a very bitter experience of life
When you face humans who never apologize
Education is the most treasured gift for all
It makes you rise and never fall
The lessons are taught with sincerity
More than half take it lightly
Etiquette is absent in some
Either they are men, women and children
Some should remain mute
Because when they speak, they rebuke
Back-biting and intervening is their business
They think it is a way to success
The nation will take centuries to progress
If a few literates are still illiterates

# 25. Double Zero

00

When my son reached Intermediate
I wanted him to choose a subject appropriate
I told him to choose Chemistry
But he was interested in Business Studies

I wanted him to learn chemical reactions
But he was interested in business establishments
The first semester made me outrageous
He got a double zero out of hundred

That very moment I surrendered
I didn't want his life to be plundered
The path of knowledge leads to endless options
No need for strange combinations

All are not born with the same temperament
It is better to choose right than to get a compartment
Every single subject has its vitality
It has its justification and reasonability

Don't torture yourself by choosing the wrong
Read the book that makes you strong.

# 26. Respect

Reasons there may be many to misbehave

Engaged you are in strange deeds

Suppression is required at times

People need to stay away from the impolite

Enhance yourself and learn values

Citizen, you will become who will live with pride

Treat yourself once you become dignified

# 27. A Spoonful of Honey

Our mannerism depends on the happenings and mishappenings

The grief lies in the tongue that's sharpening

One needs to give an ear to the occurrence

Don't ever take a rapid decision

The language was invented to make communication smoother

It was implemented to have a flow of goodness

But the misery lies in the fact

It has chosen a different passage

Pleasant words are spoken by few

Harsh words are told by so many

Abusive words are also in plenty

More than half the mankind requires a spoonful of honey

The spoken words should be sweet

Don't ever let the coarseness meet

Solve your predicaments with charming words

The obscene conversation is like garbage

Let the terms flow out like the sylvan flowers

Let the discussion be as cool as the dazzling stars.

# 28. EXTROVERt

Example you must set for others

Xenomania you must become

Talk and let others speak too

Rise from the slumber

Outrageous will pull you down

Vivacious will help you out

Expect the unexpected in return

Relax and manipulate the world

Trust is the most vital thing to be gained

# 29. Comparison

You will remain you
I will remain I
No one should take a trial
God has made everyone special
Our thoughts vary
Our looks vary
What you like I dislike
You are calm I am loquacious
You love to laugh
I like to sit and cry
You relish vegetables
I enjoy chocolates
You sip hot tea
While I cold coffee
Two people always stand apart
Every individual is aloof and smart
It is better not to make a comparison
It may lead to a wrong decision.

# 30. Seriousness

Someday you will outshine others

Everlasting should be your decisions

Rivers of blissfulness would flow

Interest should not vary anyhow

Outstanding will be your performance

Understand the things deeply

Smile and do it patiently

Never give way to dependency

Exactness will automatically come

Sunshine will be in plenty

Success will follow soon

# 31. Puff Or Sip

College life has begun
Every student is on the run
Now the friends hold a primary place
Parents are shifted to a secondary place

The peer pressure and the mood swings
They start indulging in strange dealings
The curiosity to discover is at its peak
To become a superman or superwoman is at its height

Like a huge rock, you stand in the middle
Your life is almost a riddle
In this choice either you survive or deprive
There are several reasons to stay alive

You take a deep puff and exhale circles in the air
You take a sip and you get intoxicated
The puff and sip will lead to devastation
Don’t take advantage of your parents’ liberation

# 32. The Boundaries and the Walls

Born in whichever land you are
Let the boundaries and the walls be dear
Love the traditions and customs of your territory
We come to know about them through history
The place which gives you identity
If you stay faithful it will give you dignity
Your heart should bleed for your country
Let the people stay courageously
It will be the kingdom of your dreams
Where you will accomplish your passions
You should save yourself from falling in a stream
By striving to make it a land of your dreams
Save your nation from every danger
Rise from hatred and throw the anger
Never let the foe conquer you
Sit not idle but fight through and through
Patriotism is an inborn spirit
Never let it go till your last minute.

# 33. Optimistic

Often, we come across negativity

Positivity gives us authenticity

Time never remains the same

Illumine the world with a bright flame

Mundane thoughts lead to dullness

Impartial should be the judgments

Sarcastic remarks should not be given

Tune your thoughts generously

Idealistic theories must be set

Contrast leads to distress

# 34. Canvas

True love may blossom anytime
It may be in school or in college time
Exchanging messages and glances
You may get many chances
Your relationship may grow with each new class
It can be beautifully painted on a canvas
Let love be as pure as the driven snow
The path of faithfulness you should follow
Let it be as transparent as the looking glass
The class conflicts may make it weak
It is better to become mild and speak
The elders should generously comprehend
The differences in caste should end
There are times when they fail to agree
This leads the lovers to flee
Then they tumble down the slope
They think it is better to cope.

# 35. PUNCTUALITY

Perfection is the basic need of the date

Utmost times you have reached late

Neglecting some serious assignments

Catch it up before it's too late

Time is and always will be precious

Understand the concepts and be serious

Active you should be in all aspects of life

Life becomes smooth if you are punctual

It leads to success in a manner gradual

Train your mind to do things in time

Yelling will never make you reach your destiny in time

# 36. Work is Worship

If in this universe we need to survive

We need to work day and night

Every human being is a master in some

He will thrive on the money wholesome

Some work for pleasure others for leisure

Some are workaholics others unperturbed

There are utmost choices in work in your life

Try your best to make it finite

Do it with diligence and regularity

Make it always a priority

Build such a relationship with your work
So that it doesn't seem to be like a job
Let your work sail smoothly as a ship
Sincerely consider that work is worship.

# 37. Value Relationships

The world has now taken a new pace
Where money holds a prominent place
The journey to earn wealth is endless
Some handfuls want it less

Industriousness brings success to all
Either they are major or minor in all
Let not your mind be engrossed with wealth
Let not relationships suffer due to affluence

There may be times when you have plenty
At times you are left with scanty
Brothers' sisters, parents or relatives
Abandon them never for the sake of money

Let not materialism kill the modern man
Value relationships to become an outstanding man.

# 38. Hidden Talent

Every single soul on this earth is blessed
It has in it something suppressed
Gently we get to comprehend the world
We are clueless of the interest we may hold
It may be a book, it may be a star
It may be a bird, it may be a flower
The passions grow up with the years
There is plenty of time to ponder
Imitation never brings satisfaction
It leads to your inner devastation
Follow your interests sincerely
Then you analyze it more deeply
'Don't be envious of other persons popularity
Your passion should develop with clarity
Stand in the meadows and smell the fragrance
Take a walk and go for a hunt
Discover and prosper your hidden talent.

# 39. The Winner

Countless thoughts always occupy our mind
How to bring up our children in the present time
As an infant, the child is a stranger
Days and nights have no differences any longer
From an infant, he grows up as a toddler
He learns the first steps to climb
The child is innocent and has little desires
Teach the child to firmly hold the pencil
He is now an adolescent
They start learning the art of conversation
They will follow your words and speech
Try to be selective in what you teach
Then he climbs the next step
To become a teenager at its best
Every day his actions are different
All these you must carefully handle
In inculcating, values do not mishandle
The parents who sacrifice their time for children

They are the ones who make them a gem
When you notice your kids blossoming
You remember the day you taught them a lesson
The winner you will prove to be in all aspects
Your children will always bring you respect.

# 40. Teaching

Teacher is the most dignified person on earth

Examination you must clear for a reason

Artistic and presentable in every field

Choose the subject you love to teach

Honour all the literates you meet

Ignore all the illiterates

Note down the valuable points and discuss

Guide your students to read and not to make a fuss

*Section 3*

# ENCHANTING HAIKU

# 41. Amazing Plan

His amazing plan

is perfect in every sense

I truly believe

# 42. Live for Others

It is very easy

only to live for yourself

live for others too

# 43. Raindrops

Let the raindrops fall

you can hide the tears of pain

in the cold droplets

# 44. Live in Present

Make way for good

leave the sincere past behind

live in the present

# 45. Survive

We grow with nature

it helps us to survive in

all circumstances

# 46. Moon

Off-white moon at night

changes its shape every day

providing calmness

# 47. Magic

Magic has begun

you understand me truly

now, I don't know-how

# 48. The View Breathtaking

The view breathtaking

with the hills, valleys and gorges

I am stuck in-between

# 49. Reaching Heaven

I follow your path

let there be no obstacles

In reaching heaven

# 50. Love Your Silence

I love your silence

beautiful untouched damsel

but your lips quiver

# 51. Rainbow

Rainbow in the sky

its hues radiate the sky

as well as the earth

# 52. Broken but I Rise

Broken but I rise

ever ready to compromise

adjustments follow

# 53. A Stray Dog

A stray dog

feed them if it is hungry

a thick slice of bread

# 54. Charitable

If you be wealthy

try to be charitable

serve the destitute

# 55. Give Abundant Time

Give abundant time

to the ones you give birth to

make them generous

# 56. Music

My ears breathe music

my heart dances on the tunes

then I swirl around

# 57. Lotus

Sign of purity

the pink lotus in the pond

of impure water

# 58. Sea- Shore

The evening sea tides

washing the dirt from the shore

leaving cleanliness

# 59. The Night Jasmine

The Night Jasmine tree
the fragrance so mystical
brought from Paradise

# 60. The Falcon

Displaying wisdom

the Falcon a sign of freedom

strength and victory

# *Section 4*

# APPEALING

# 61. The Art of Becoming Beautiful

There is not a sole human being in this world
Who doesn't want to look charismatic at all
As we ripen, we exhibit ourselves
We master the art of looking seductive
One day these false notions will show up
In several activities, we must pause
We easily please ourselves and others
We make a thousand men suffer
If our faults exceed in number
The face becomes blank and insecure
The heart becomes infected and impure
What is the art of becoming beautiful?
It happens when you become trustworthy and dutiful
If you follow the path of sacredness
Your face will have an aura of holiness
It will reflect your generosity

There will be no more complexity
So let your face become one in a million
It will become as bright as vermilion.

# 62. Greens and Purples

Nature has bestowed us with foods galore

Have a look at what the body has in store

To live a life free from diseases

You have to gulp down healthy dishes

To develop a lithe and handsome body

Have your vitamins and calcium properly

Proteins and minerals are to be taken daily

If you don't follow the deficiencies are scary

You may remain grieved and never be merry

Have your greens and your purples

To save yourself from wrinkles

Let sugar and salt intake be in limited quantity

It will keep you away from depression and anxiety

Love your body and do the daily exercises

So that you may lead your life free from diseases.

# 63. Life Partner

Let us be drenched in the rain
Let us make our lives ecstatic again
I want to feel the droplets on my body
I want to sing for you a rhapsody
We have felt each other's presence for years
The hullabaloo of life kept us apart

You were striving day and night
To make our lives flawless and radiant
The children have grown with us
Now they no longer live with us
You and I are together again
Let there be no bargain
You are with me now
I am forever with you now
Let us begin our life anew
There is a strange tranquillity between us now
It depicts our maturity anyhow
As a life partner, you are beyond comparison
I want to spend my life with the one I had chosen.

# 64. Flair for Reading

We commence with our A B C

We come up to joining these in letters one, two or three

Alphabets to words and then to sentences

In this manner our learning advances

In school and college, we learn our subjects

After that, we never look back but rather neglect

The most extraordinary quality you should develop

A habit for lifelong with which you should come up

It is to have a flair for reading the scholars

Thousands of contributors have shared their experiences

They have penned down in several languages

Each one carries a special message

It depends on how you access

Each poem, story, novel or an essay

Read with interest as it carries an essence

Exposure to history or gist of culture

Steps to morality and modernism in literature

Every line is meaningful and spectacular

Reading takes you away from the absurdities of life

You enter a new world of surprises

Innumerable writers have left marvellous works

Let us pay respect to these men of letters.

# 65. Nine More Months

On the first day when you entered the womb
I got to know you very soon
I was to have strange experiences
We were elated with the expectations
Inside me, a tiny seed was growing
I could feel my mood swinging
My blood was running in your veins
It was I who will bear the pain
I could feel you tossing and tumbling
My steps had started stumbling
Your heart was beating inside me
You were so close to me
I was a blessed woman on earth
I was about to give birth
The immense pain continued for hours
Your birth would certainly change my stars
My pain melted like thin ice
The moment I saw you smile

Lying next to me was my bundle of joy
Tears rolled down and I wanted to cry
For nine more months, we are related to one another
I was on top of the world as I had become a mother.

# 66. Saviour

It is believed that millions of years ago
In the universe, a serene air did flow
Countless valleys flowed among the hills
The animals in the open did thrill

Human beings had no language
They had no sense of being candid
There was no education or qualification
They were free from power and position

The gradual development followed
The human brain stands exposed
Marvellous experiments are done
More than half the world is on the run

Today the world beholds the new sight
Human beings have reached great heights
At times there is chaos and destruction
No matter how strong may be the foundation?

This is a call for the coming generation
Save nature if you want to grow your nation
Act as a saviour, not a destroyer
Let the world bloom like a beautiful flower.

# 67. Definition of Love

Love is a passion and desire
It burns the heart with fire
Every child receives the utmost love from parents
We teach them to love their siblings
Let us teach them the art of love
Let love survive and hate subside
Let love be unconditional
Do not calculate it with riches
It will then leave you as a dummy
Desires are spreading their roots
It is crushing adoration under its boots
Let us change the definition of love
Let the mind be virtuous with the thoughts of love
Make it pure and serene as the heaven above.

# 68. Four Seasons

Millions of years ago a man was born with a reason
He had to adapt himself in the natural surroundings
To let the earth, breathe, God planned the four seasons
Spring, summer, autumn and winter have a special bonding

**Spring** months come with their customs
The Sun gives little warmth in this season
A serene air flows and the trees shed their leaves
It is a time of rebirth and rejuvenation

**Summer** months come out with a blow
The hottest and least awaited in the row
The red-hot sun is at its peak with sunshine
It is a time of dryness, waterless and brittleness

**Autumn** months have their significance
The leaves in shades of yellow and red
Traditions and festivities are in full swing
They are the months of transition

**Winter** months are whiter than white

The season is cold due to the chilly winds that blow

The frost, snowfall and the dense fog

The blossoming petunias, pansies, and the dianthus.

# 69. My First Crush

Those days when I was gaining puberty
My thoughts were still gaining maturity
I moved in and I moved out
I looked at the mirror and made a pout
Parents believed dressing up was a crime
They wanted education to be worthwhile
I lived in a dream world of my own
With the mere thought of handsome boys, I was blown
Some cute others lithesome
Some still shy while others dumb
Who will be the one to move my heart?
This question aroused in my mind day and night
My first crush was still out of sight
Finally, one day my heart did burst
When I realized that it was my first crush
I adored the way he conversed
I loved the way he walked
His every action made my heart swing

In my ears, only his voice did ring
This crush always remains a hidden aspect
In the corner of your heart, it is placed lifelong
A dream with which you will cherish off and on.

# 70. Heaven on Earth-Kashmir

In the north of India stands an admirable place

Some five centuries ago it attained grace

It settled in the eyes of the Mughals

They kept the state free from rivals

They flourished every nook and corner

Jahangir was mesmerized by its serenity

The crystal-clear water of Dal and Nageen Lake

The gentle flow of the Jhelum River

The snowcapped mountains peaks touching the clouds

The heights of glorious Gulmarg hills

The silent drizzle on the tracks of Pahalgam

The mystical leaves of the Chinar trees

To Nur Jahan the light of his world

He gifted the delightful Shalimar Bagh

On seeing the beauty he said " Agar Firdaus ba roy zamin ast,

Hamin ast-u hamin ast-u hamin ast"

(If there is Paradise on earth, it is this it is this it is this)
Srinagar in Kashmir the city of wealth
Srinagar in Kashmir the city of the sun
The hills and the valleys still stand untouched
The houseboats carry an aura of hospitality
The nine bridges a touch of modernity
Our country is blessed with this heaven on earth.

# 71. My Country India

To the country which I belong

The land is blessed, and I go headstrong

Siachin in Kashmir is in the Northernmost

Kanya Kumari is in the southernmost

Kibithu village of Arunachal Pradesh in Easternmost

Ghuar Mota of Kutch in the Westernmost

It stretches itself with all its zest

Twenty-eight states with Union territories eight

With languages twenty two which are spoken in these states

Famine and drought are miles away

The twelve rivers flow in full swing and sway

The Ganga, the Yamuna and the Saraswati

Pass through states and enter the ocean with gaiety

The Arabian Sea in the South West and Bay of Bengal in the South East

The Indian Ocean in the South beats the rest

The capital is Delhi a metropolitan city

Mumbai being the largest city

The nation with all its glory feels high

The tri-coloured flag with a chakra touches the sky

The colours saffron, white, blue and green

Enhances the nation with all its sheen

The blushing pink Lotus is the National flower

The dancing Peafowl exhibits itself as the National bird

The Pumpkin with all its vitamins the National vegetable

The ferocious Bengal Tiger the National animal

The delicious mangoes the National fruit

Hockey being the National Sport

It is the country which breathes with history

With Taj Mahal and the Golden Temple as the glimpses of beauty

Holy is the land with the birth of the blessed ones

Where Hinduism, Sikhism, Jainism, and Buddhism began

Temples, Gurudwaras, Churches and Mosques

Throng with worshippers of various castes

Democracy being the greatest boon

All men and women enjoy their rights late or soon

Let our hearts be full of patriotism every minute

Let us sing the song with a National spirit

The National song **Vande Mataram by Bankim Chandra Chaterjee**

The National anthem **Jana Gana Mana by Rabindranath Tagore**

This is my country India which I adore.

# 72. Mumtaj Mahal

An everlasting Persian beauty betrothed to Shahjahan

Was bestowed with the title of Mumtaz Mahal Begum

The exalted one of the palaces was she

Profound love between them was carefree

Just after nineteen years of marriage, she breathed her last

The death of his partner left him depressed

He wanted his woman to live with her forever

He planned to build a tomb for her

The marvellous Crown of the Palace was built

An ivory-white mausoleum in Agra

It was built on the banks of Yamuna River

Twenty thousand artisans beautified it

Twenty years it took for completion

Surrounded by lush green gardens and fountains

It is a place next to heaven

An example of the deep love he had set in this world

He got two tombs in memory of his love

Both lie in the grave next to each other

The monument will speak the story of their love forever.

# 73. Ocean of Love

In every nook and corner, I see love birds hanging
They think love is just a happening
The immature and innocent teenagers
Making misuse of parents' liberation
It takes decades for love to grow
Still, you may not fathom each other though
You decide to live life long
There may be dissimilarities and hard to get along
Love bonding may create disturbances
While facing reality it may create nuances
So, let the process of love be gradual
Let the ocean of love flow in the individuals
The day you accept each other's pros and cons
That very day you will see a new dawn.

# 74. Father Son

The day he starts wearing your boots

Take a pause but don't stay mute

As a **Father** you silently observe

At times you succeed and at times you lose

There has never been a scarcity of love

You are harsh but with a motive

You never want him to be a failure

You always want him to be an achiever

The time has come to remove the generation gap

Try to be a cool and calm dad

Let him speak up and not hide secret deep down

Give him profound love he is your son

As a **Son,** you have grown with him

Step by step you follow him

His every action and conversation

Makes an impact on your relation

You abhor him when he gets angry

At times you disobey and become unhappy

One day you grow up and leave him

He may never ask you to spend on him

You are bright as the sunshine

He always wants you to outshine

Learn to love and give him the utmost care

Give him profound love he is your father.

# 75. On the Death of My Dog

They brought him in a small basket
He was tiny, fawn coloured and looked classic
His wrinkly face and flat nose
He kept turning his head as if making a pose
Such a lovely dog with protruding eyes
He made his way in everyone's heart
With his small four feet, he danced around
The floor was not made for him indeed
He cuddled on a sofa or a bed with ease
He fumbled with all the visitors
A peck on the cheek was for all
He lived a life full of comfort
For almost twenty hours he snored
One fine morning it was a devastating sight
When the two dogs had a serious fight
The left eye of Dollar was hanging
A stream of blood was flowing

The other dog got a good thrashing

His eye was stitched and put in place

He lost his attraction and grace

His moaning was heart-rending

We never wanted this to happen

For twenty days he suffered a lot

One evening he silently breathed his last

Tears started running down our eyes

His soul must have reached heaven in the skies

His memories will keep coming with the summer and winter fog

This is a sad song on the death of my dog.

# 76. Seduction

Silently you enter the nerves of the brain

Engage yourself in pleasure and pain

Dancing and singing to please others

Ubiquitous is your presence

Control yourself and take a pause

Tingling sensations you give to many

Illicit relationships you may develop

Overflowing with enormous love

Notorious you become anyhow

# 77. My Christmas Tree

Throughout the year I nurture the pine

In December, it begins to shine

On every Christmas Eve, I place it in the living room

Then I begin to decorate it soon

With metal balls, gifts and silver bells

With Candy canes and chocolates hanging with ribbons

A silver star I place on the treetop

The Christmas tree lights brighten my room

The tree looks magical and mystical

The bells on it begin to jingle

On every starry Christmas night

Santa Claus comes on the sledge

He places a special gift near my Christmas tree in the night

He removes all the wrongs and does the right.

# 78. Grandparents

Your warm wrinkled hands wake me up in the morning

You touch my forehead gently to give a blessing

I feel so cosy in your warm lap

I love to hear fables and I clap

You hug me tight when I get a scolding

You console me when I am grieved and longing

Your life has been full of experiences

Step by step you help me in developing

You sit and feed me when I am hungry

You teach me to be happy when I am angry

I have received enormous love from my parents

But the love of Grandparents is beyond comparison

# 79. I Will Keep on Loving You

I don't care for the differences that may arise
I know you are sincerely honest and wise
For me, you are one among the few
I will keep on loving you

The word pessimism does not exist in my dictionary
The word optimism holds a senior degree
Let my noble thoughts not stand in a queue
I will keep on loving you

At times I stumble down and fall
You are there to nurture me in your cell
On the canvas of my life, I have drawn you
I will keep on loving you

My life is black and white

I look up to you when forlorn and depressed

Our relationship grows and you prove to be true

I will keep on loving you.

# 80. Appealing

Alluring is your look from head to toe

Passionate with every friend and foe

Positivity brings energy though

Enchanting is your bower

Anxious to be with your loved ones

Love may be true or false

Instantaneous should be the reaction anyhow

Neglect the ones who defame you

Gorgeous you will be with such attributes

Dr Harmeet Kaur Bhalla
Kanpur